Someday Heaven

WRITTEN BY
Larry Libby

ILLUSTRATED BY
Wayne McLoughlin

Zonderkidz

Someday Heaven
Copyright © 2001 by Larry Libby
Illustrations copyright © 2001 by Wayne McLoughlin

Requests for information should be addressed to:

Zonderkidz
The children's group of Zondervan

Grand Rapids, Michigan 49530
www.zonderkidz.com

Zonderkidz is a trademark of The Zondervan.

ISBN 0-310-70105-8

Library of Congress Cataloging-in-Publication Data
Libby, Larry.
Someday Heaven / written by Larry Libby.
        p. cm.
ISBN 0-310-70105-8
1. Heaven-Christianity-Juvenile literature.
2. Future life-Christianity-Juvenile literature. [1. Heaven. 2. Future life. 3. Christian life.] I. Title.
BT849 .L53 2000
 236'.24—dc21   0-068522

Editors: Etta Wilson, Gwen Ellis
Art Direction and Design: Michelle Lenger, Amy Peterman

Printed in Malaysia
02 03 04 / 5 4

for my family,
Laura, Matthew, and Melissa

If I get to heaven first,
I'll scout out the best hiking trails.
I love you.

Introduction

Have you ever watched the clouds when the sun slips low in the sky? The blue of the sky washes away into crimson and pink and purple. The big billowy clouds ride high and proud into the coming night and sometimes ... sometimes before you see the first little star ... you can almost see castles and great houses in the clouds. You can almost imagine the setting sun shining gold and red on heaven's high windows.

Does God's home look like that? Where does God live? Is he ever lonesome? Does he like having company? Will he take me to his home someday ... after I die? What will it be like?

We have so many questions about heaven. The Bible tells us just a little, and we need to understand what it says. The Bible makes it clear that God wants to welcome us to his forever home. What a wonderful place heaven must be!

Where Is Heaven?

The Bible says that heaven is up. When God looks at earth from heaven, he looks down. When Jesus left earth to go back to heaven, he went up until he disappeared into a cloud.

Jesus didn't need a stairway. He just lifted his hands and up he went. The people who were with Jesus scrunched up their eyes and stared into the sky. They watched as he rose higher and higher in the air, like a balloon that floats so high in the wind, it looks like a tiny silver speck in the wide blue.

Heaven is a real place, and it is up. But where? Is heaven a perfect planet, far away in a distant galaxy? Is heaven tucked away in some secret corner of space? The Bible doesn't say. But Jesus did tell us one thing: he is the only way to get there!

From heaven the LORD looks down and sees everyone. From his throne he watches all those who live on the earth.
Psalm 33:13-14

How Do I Get to Heaven?

The way to heaven isn't a road. It isn't a path. It isn't a street. It's a *Person*.

Jesus is the stairway to heaven. Jesus is the door. Jesus is the only way anyone ever finds heaven.

This is hard to understand, even for grown-ups. But it reminds me of a little boy I know—a boy with a very strong big brother. One day the little boy looked way up in a tree and saw his big brother sitting on a limb.

"I wish I could climb up there," the boy said.

"Come on up," said his brother.

"I can't," said the boy. "My arms aren't strong enough. I could never climb that tree."

"Yes, you can!" said his big brother.

And do you know what happened? The big brother slid down the tree, put his little brother on his back, and shinnied back up the tree to that big limb.

"Now," said the big brother, "you can be with me where I am." And they sat together on that fine, high limb, just as happy as a couple of birds.

That's what Jesus has done for us. We could never climb up to where he lives. We could never open heaven's door by our own hard work.

But God wants us there! That's why Jesus came all the way down from heaven to show us the way. Only he is strong enough and good enough to open heaven's door and take us inside.

Jesus answered, "I am the way and the truth and the life.
No one comes to the Father except through me."
John 14:6

How Long Does It Take to Get to Heaven?

It may not take any longer than closing your eyes on earth—and opening them up in heaven! When the Lord Jesus was put on a cross to die, two men who had done bad things were put on crosses too. One was on one side, and one was on the other.

One of the men turned his head toward Jesus and looked into his eyes.

Then the man said, "Jesus, remember me when you come into your kingdom!"

Jesus answered him, "What I am about to tell you is true. Today you will be with me in paradise" (Luke 23:43).

Within a few hours Jesus and both of the men died. And on that very day, Jesus and the man who had prayed to him on the cross were both in heaven!

Did you ever fall asleep in the living room watching TV, eating cookies, and drinking milk, and then wake up in the morning in your warm bed? How do you think that happened? Well, let me tell you. When you fell asleep, someone carried you gently into your bedroom. Without even waking you up, your mother or your father put pajamas on you, tucked you into bed, and left you to sleep all night long.

That's similar to what the Lord does for us when we die. We fall asleep down here on earth and wake up in God's house!

Who Lives in Heaven?

If heaven had a phone book, how big do you think it would be? And whose names would be in the book?

If you looked under the letter G, I guess you'd find the name "God the Father." He doesn't need a telephone, of course, but he does like people to call him.

You could look under J and find "Jesus." He has always lived in heaven. But he also lived here on earth for a time.

You could look under H and find "Holy Spirit." He is the helper who lives inside everyone who loves Jesus. He is in heaven too.

You would see lots and lots of other names. Names of brave men and women who gave up their homes and even their lives for Jesus. Names of parents and children who loved God and obeyed his Word even when the whole world turned against them.

Jesus said that whoever believes in him will have his or her name written down in a book in heaven. It isn't a phone book. It's called the Book of Life, and it is very big. Your name is in that book if you believe in Jesus. You can be sure of that!

"Call out to me. I will answer you. I will tell you
great things you do not know."
Jeremiah 33:3

How Long Will I Be in Heaven?

When you're at your best friend's house, laughing and playing, time goes by so fast that you can hardly believe it. Zip! Whizz! The hands seem to fly around the clock. Maybe you can remember saying in your heart, *Oh, this day is so good. I wish it could last forever!*

That's what heaven is. It's a good day that lasts forever.

Really, time won't go fast or slow, because there will be no time at all in heaven! If you stopped an angel and said, "Please, what time is it?" The angel would just laugh and say, "Why, it's right now and it's forever."

Jesus will see to all that. And even though Jesus may be the busiest person in all of heaven, he will never be too busy to laugh with you or sail a boat with you or go for a walk with you. Do you know what he said? He said, "I am always with you" (Matthew 28:20).

And when our Lord Jesus makes a promise, he will never break it.

Will It Always Be Light in Heaven?

I know a little boy who couldn't sleep unless his mom or dad left the hall light on. He didn't like the dark. But the soft light coming from the hall shone into his bedroom and helped him snuggle down in his covers and fall asleep. That boy would be glad to know about the light in heaven.

Our forever home won't need the sun and moon. It won't need starlight or streetlights or flashlights or night-lights. The Lord God will be all the light we will ever need. So there will be no darkness to be afraid of in heaven. There will be no darkness to end our fun or cloud our eyes or cast the smallest shadow over our happiness.

Until we begin to enjoy heaven's always-light, the Bible can help us see the way we ought to go, the things we ought to do, and the words we ought to say. The Bible is like a bright, burning lamp that chases back the shadows and shows us where to walk.

Isn't God good to give us some light until we get to heaven?

Your word is like a lamp that shows me the way.
It is like a light that guides me.
Psalm 119:105

Will Anyone Meet Me
When I Get to Heaven?

When you go visit your best friends, isn't it great to see them waiting for you? When you get home from school, doesn't it make you feel good to be met at the door by your mom—especially if she's baked some cookies? When you go to your grandparents' house, isn't it fun to see them watching for you through the front window?

When people love you, they watch and wait for you. Arriving in heaven will be like coming home to the warm welcome of loved ones.

Maybe the people who will smile the biggest welcome will be the ones who prayed for you and taught you about Jesus. How happy they will be to see that you gave your life to the Lord!

If someone you love is already in heaven, he or she may be watching for you. And when you walk smiling through that doorway, how happy your loved one will be.

Who will be the happiest? You can guess that one. That's right. Jesus will be happiest of all. Don't you think he will be the first one to hug you when you step into heaven? And I know what he will say: "Come in! Come in! I've been waiting for you!"

Will There Be Other
Children in Heaven?

Will there be children in heaven? Children playing games with angels? Children running and skipping and turning cartwheels around the feet of Jesus as he walks with them?

The Bible tells us some very important things Jesus said about children and heaven.

One day some parents were bringing their girls and boys to Jesus so he could put his hands on them and pray for them. The Lord's followers tried to stop them. They said something like, "Don't bother the Lord! He doesn't have time for a bunch of noisy, squirmy kids. Go away!"

What do you suppose Jesus thought about that? He said something that surprised his followers very much: "Let the little children come to me. Don't keep them away. God's kingdom belongs to people like them" (Mark 10:14). Then he took the children in his arms. He put his hands on them and blessed them.

Just as Jesus loved those children, he loves children all over the world today. Children who trust Jesus as their Lord and Savior will be in heaven. We don't know if they will be young or old once they get there. It isn't important. The important thing is that they will be with Jesus forever and ever.

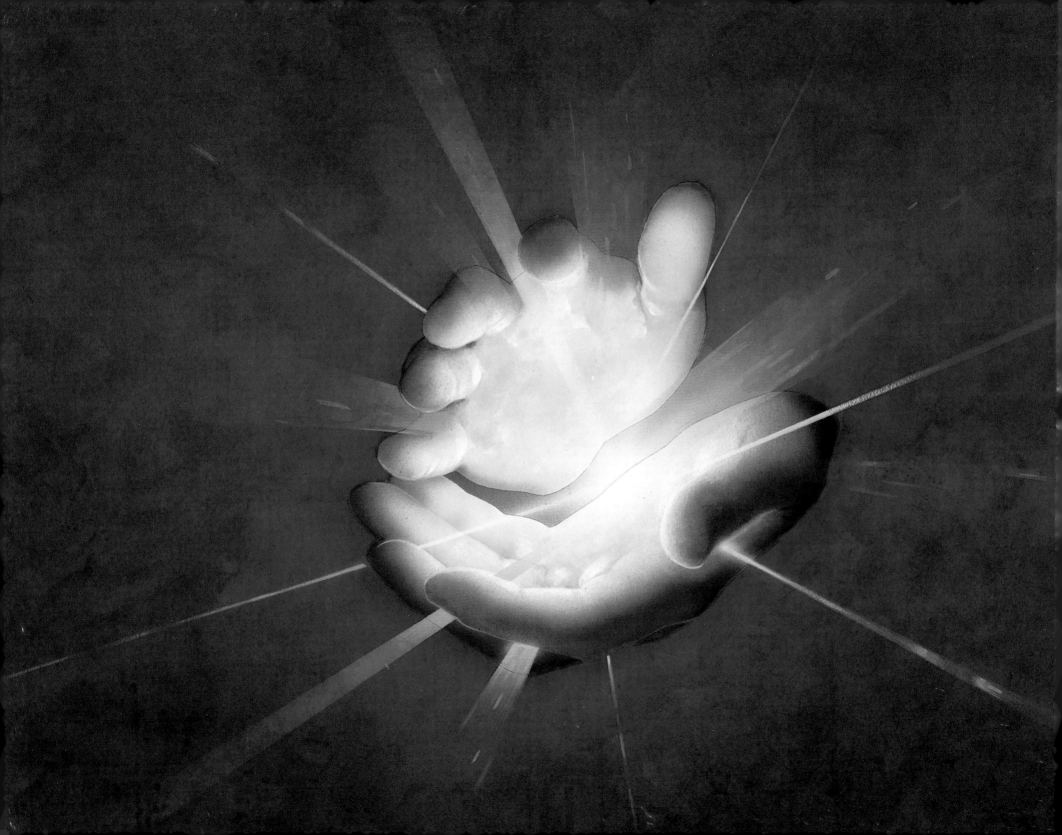

Will I Be an Angel
When I Get to Heaven?

No, you won't be an angel. You will be yourself! People and angels are both creations of God, but they are very different. And they will continue to be different in heaven too. God created lots and lots of angels way back in the beginning. God enjoyed them very much, and they serve him with glad hearts.

But even after he created the beautiful angels who sang and praised him and shone like stars bursting for joy—even after that—God had something more in his heart. He wanted to create again.

The angels, wide-eyed with delight, must have watched him as he scooped the dirt into his hands and gently formed the first man who ever lived. Later on he took one of Adam's ribs and made a woman. God loved these people very much, just as he loved the angels.

So when you get to heaven, you will probably meet angels who will nudge one another and say, "Look! There is one of those special people that the Lord Jesus saved for himself!"

And just maybe you will get the chance to sit down with one or two of them in a field of flowers beside a golden road and hear all about heaven.

Will I Need
Money in Heaven?

You will have all that you need in your forever home. And you can begin right now putting lots and lots of treasure into the Bank of Heaven. Jesus talked about heavenly treasure. He said we ought to store up heavenly treasure that will last. He also said it was a lot better to have riches in heaven than a bunch of money piled up here on earth. We put treasure in heaven by doing good deeds and by sharing what we have with others.

What does treasure in heaven look like? Is it green paper money? I don't think so. We won't have to pay for anything in our Father's house. Jesus paid it all.

Will heaven's treasure be in gold coins? I don't think so. What good would they be? If the streets are paved with gold, then gold will be as common as sand on a thousand long beaches.

Will heaven's money be beautiful jewels? Probably not. The heavenly city will be full of more sparkling, flashing jewels than you could ever count.

Heaven's treasure won't be stacks of paper money. It won't be gold. It won't be jewels. What will this treasure be?

God doesn't tell us what it looks like. But he does say we can begin saving now. And he says we'll be glad we did!

Put away riches for yourselves in heaven. There, moths and rust
do not destroy them. There, thieves do not break in and steal them.
Your heart will be where your riches are.
Matthew 6:20-21

Will I Ever Be
Sad in Heaven?

The Bible says that when we first get to heaven, God will wipe away all our tears. And then it says, "There will be no more death or sadness. There will be no more crying or pain" (Revelation 21:4).

Will there be a little sadness left when we first step into heaven? Could there be a few hurts that haven't been soothed away? If we have just slipped through the doorway called "death," perhaps we may feel sad about the pain we felt or for the people we had to leave behind.

Who will comfort us? God himself! He will softly wipe the tears from our eyes. He may whisper, "Don't cry. You're home now! Everything will be all right. I am with you always, and now you will always be with me."

By the time he has wiped away our tears and held us close for a while, the sadness will all be gone. And it will never come back again.

Sobbing can remain through the night.
But joy comes in the morning.
Psalm 30:5

Will My Grandpa Still
Be Old in Heaven?

Your grandpa will have a brand-new body in heaven. His back won't hurt him when he gets up in the morning. He won't need glasses. He won't need a hearing aid. He won't have to walk with a cane.

The Bible says that the bodies we have on earth aren't the right kind to live forever. They wear out, like your favorite sneakers or your brother's old bicycle. We get to trade in our old bodies for new ones. And how wonderful our new bodies will be! They won't get tired or need sleep. They won't get hurt or have aches and pains. They'll be able to run and run and run and never grow tired.

You've never seen your grandpa like that! Even your grandma, who met him when he was young and full of energy, never saw him like that! He will be like Jesus. He will never get sick again. He won't have to take pills. He won't ever feel bad or need operations.

And if your grandpa is already in heaven, he will never have to grow old and die again.

Will My Pets
Go to Heaven?

Our wise Creator must have had such a good time creating animals. God knew just what he was doing when he made kittens soft and playful, and hamsters shy and whiskery. And can't you imagine God smiling when he designed the face of a dog? It was God who gave dogs their cold noses, soft droopy ears, funny faces, and floppy tongues.

After God had created all the animals in the world, he said, "It is *good!*"

But because death came when sin entered the world way back at the beginning, all the animals and all the people in the world have to die. The Bible says that after death, people live forever. But the Bible doesn't say if animals live forever. If they do, God has decided not to tell us.

But wouldn't it be a wonderful surprise to get to heaven and find the strangest and cuddliest and friendliest and grandest animals that you have ever seen! Our God loves surprises. And who knows? Maybe he will surprise us with the pets we loved on earth. Our God can do anything!

How Can I Know for Sure That I'm Going to Heaven?

Going to heaven is so important, you want to be very, very sure that it's where you'll be going when the time comes to leave this life. And you can be sure. You don't have to wonder. You don't have to be afraid or worry.

Jesus came all the way from heaven to show us the way. When you know that you believe in him and are ready to give your life to Jesus, you might say a prayer to him like this:

"Dear Lord Jesus, thank you for inviting me to your beautiful forever home. Thank you for inviting me to be a child of God. Thank you for bleeding and dying on the cross for all the bad, hurtful things I have done. I want to belong to you. I want you to be Lord and King of my life. Please forgive me for the bad things in my heart. Please come into my life and be with me always. Amen."

If you prayed that prayer, then be happy, because someday we'll all be together with Jesus in heaven forever. And that is something to *really* be happy about!

Jesus said, "Anyone who hears my word and believes him who sent me has eternal life. He will not be found guilty. He has crossed over from death to life."
John 5:24